LOBSTERS

Gangsters of the Sea

LOBSTERS
Gangsters of the Sea

TEXT BY
Mary M. Cerullo

PHOTOGRAPHS BY
Jeffrey L. Rotman

COBBLEHILL BOOKS
Dutton   New York

The photograph on page 22 is by Dr. Jelle Atema of the Boston University Marine Program of the Marine Biological Laboratory, Woods Hole, Massachusetts. Diagram on page 24 courtesy University of Maine Sea Grant Marine Advisory Program.

Library of Congress Cataloging-in-Publication Data
Cerullo, Mary M.
Lobsters : gangsters of the sea / text by Mary M. Cerullo :
photographs by Jeffrey L. Rotman.
p.   cm.
Includes bibliographical references and index.
Summary: Describes the physical aspects, habits, and life cycle of the Maine lobster
as well as the activities of New England lobstermen.
ISBN 0-525-65153-5
1. American lobster—Juvenile literature.   2. American lobster—New England—
Juvenile literature.   3. Lobster fisheries—New England—Juvenile literature.
[1. Lobsters.]   I. Rotman, Jeffrey L., ill.   II. Title.
QL444.M33C47 1994 595.3'841—dc20 93-1288 CIP AC

Published in the United States by Cobblehill Books,
an affiliate of Dutton Children's Books,
a division of Penguin Books USA Inc.,
375 Hudson Street, New York, New York 10014

Designed by Charlotte Staub
Printed in Hong Kong
First Edition   10 9 8 7 6 5 4 3 2 1

Dedicated to
George and Ursula
—MMC

This one is for Ken Beck
—JLR

ACKNOWLEDGMENTS

Thank you to Dr. Jelle Atema of the Boston University Marine Program of the Marine Biological Laboratory, Woods Hole, Massachusetts; Dr. David Dow, Director of the Lobster Institute, Orono, Maine; and Robert Goode, Chairman of the Marine Science Department of Southern Maine Technical College, South Portland, for their review of the manuscript. Thanks also to Sam Chapman of the Darling Research Center in Walpole, Maine, and to Dr. Jay Krouse of the Maine Department of Marine Resources for their patient answers to many questions.

Contents

A lobster boat bucks rising seas to finish hauling traps before a storm breaks.

CHAPTER ONE

A Battle Above and a Battle Below

Leaden clouds hovered just above the white-capped waves. The seas were rising and the small lobster boat was still three miles off Portland Head Light. Bob Goode called to his sternman to hurry up with the bait bags. With luck, they'd finish hauling their last string of traps before the storm broke. He gaffed a blue and white buoy with a long hook, pulled on the line and wrapped it around a pulley connected to the hydraulic winch. It raised the trap smoothly from the water to the boat. As Bob swung the lobster pot onto the railing of his craft, he felt the first bullets of rain. He unwound the latch string that held the door of the trap closed and pried open the lid.

Inside he found a rock crab and threw it to his sternman to use to rebait the trap. Then he reached for the lobsters. One looked a bit on the small side. Bob held a brass ruler against its *carapace* or back shell. He was right. This was a "short," smaller than the legal size of 3¼ inches measured from the lobster's eye socket to the beginning of the tail. It snapped its tail vigorously in defense. Lobstermen call these small lobsters "snappers" for the energetic way they try to flip away from their captors. Bob tossed it overboard. "Come see me next year when you've grown some," he called after it.

He pulled a larger lobster from the trap. It stretched its claws wide open, spoiling for a fight. Bob deftly avoided the claws which could easily have pinched through his gloves. He banded the claws before throwing

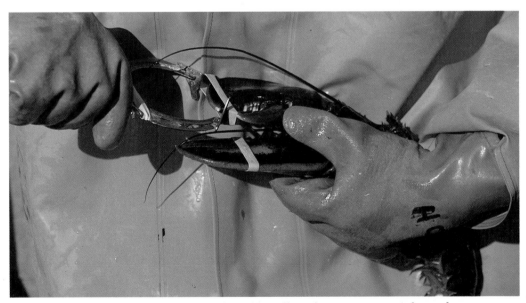

A lobsterman bands his catch as he pulls it from a trap in order to keep it from attacking other lobsters in the haul.

A pregnant lobster is easy to identify. She carries her eggs on her tail.

this one into a barrel filled with seawater. He reached into the trap again. The last lobster was also a "keeper," he figured, recognizing a legal-size lobster from many years of experience. Bob turned it on its back and grunted with displeasure when he saw the tiny "berries" glued to its tail. This was a female with eggs. She had to be returned to the sea. But before

A sternman baits a trap with redfish.

he let her go, he pulled out his knife and carved a deep V into one of her tail flippers. Even after she shed her eggs, the V-notch would caution other lobstermen that this was a good breeder. This badge of motherhood would keep her safe through several molts. For as long as she carried the mark, all lobstermen must return her to the sea. Bob released her gently back into the water.

He extracted several sea urchins, a sea cucumber, and an ocean pout —an eel-like fish. Then he passed the trap to his sternman who replaced the old bait with fresh fish heads or crabs brought up in other traps. The boat slowly steamed forward, and the rebaited traps plopped one by one back into the sea. The sternman threw the rest of the bait overboard.

Great gray herring gulls dive-bombed the discarded bait before it even hit the water. Bob Goode turned the bow of his vessel toward shore just as the full force of the storm hammered down on them.

The female lobster drifted down through the water, the turmoil of the surface behind her. She landed on the dim ocean floor, but even in the dark she quickly located a shelter. She wriggled into a crevice in the rocks and wedged her two large claws in the front of the opening. Daytime, when many predators were active, was not the time for excursions.

She remained motionless until just before nightfall. Then she slowly emerged from her shelter, prepared for a night of hunting. She encountered a large, red rock crab scuttling across the ocean floor. Exposed and vulnerable, the crab foolishly raised its claws. The lobster tore them off with barely a struggle. The female lobster carried the clawless crustacean back to the entrance to her den and buried it in her front yard. Now she wouldn't have to hunt for a few nights. She started to back into the opening when a nip on her tail informed her that someone else was already there. She whirled around to confront the intruder. A huge male stalked menacingly from the den and snapped his antennae across the smaller lobster's shell, as if to size her up. Immediately she realized that she was no match for this lobster and backed off, abandoning her home and her meal.

The scent of food drew her into shallower water. There sat another lobster pot. This time instead of crawling inside the trap, she perched on the entrance funnel and reached inside to rip off a piece of bait. She ate that and wandered on, looking for a new shelter. Nearly a mile from where she herself had been captured she dug a tunnel in the soft mud to cradle her for the day. Shortly before dawn, as the lobster was settling into sleep, Bob Goode was rousing from his.

Separated by miles of water, the lobsterman and the lobster seem to

The lobster lives in a shadowy world that helps hide it from its predators.

live in two separate worlds, but each depends on the other. The lobsterman, of course, makes his living by catching lobster. The lobster relies on the lobsterman whose traps and bait provide food. At times as much as 70 percent of the lobster's food supply comes from stealing bait from lobster traps or from scavenging bait thrown over the side at the end of a day of lobstering. This makes the lobsterman both a hunter and a farmer of the sea. To ensure his future, and the lobster's as well, the lobsterman must respect conservation laws aimed at protecting pregnant lobsters or ones too young to have reproduced. The two worlds of the lobsterman and the lobster are linked like a trap and a buoy.

A spiny lobster from the Caribbean doesn't have the large front claws of the northern American lobster.

CHAPTER TWO
The All-American Lobster

Worldwide there are many kinds of lobsters, such as crayfish, spiny lobsters, and slipper lobsters. But to the true seafood lover there is only one genuine lobster, the American lobster, *Homarus americanus*. It lives from the Canadian Maritimes down to North Carolina 1,300 miles to the south, but it is most abundant in the colder northern waters. More than half the U.S. catch of lobsters comes from the state of Maine. The lobster is so identified with the coast of Maine (it's even on the state license plate)

It is hard to tell which end is which on a tropical slipper lobster.

that Canadian lobsters being transported by truck through the state are frequently rechristened "Maine" lobsters by the time they've crossed the border into New Hampshire.

The "Maine" or American lobster is distinguished by its two strong claws: a big-toothed *crusher* claw for pulverizing shells and a finer-edged *ripper* or *pincher* claw resembling a steak knife, for tearing soft flesh. The lobster's skeleton is on the outside, which like a suit of armor protects it from its enemies. Because of the crusty covering worn by lobsters, crabs, shrimp, and barnacles, these animals are classified together as "crustaceans." Crustaceans belong to a larger group of animals called Arthropoda, which also includes spiders, insects, and horseshoe crabs.

Strong claws and a hard protective shell make the American lobster a formidable opponent. It has been called the "gangster of the sea" because it is aggressive and territorial by nature. Whenever it can, it steals bait from traps and the homes from other lobsters.

The American lobster is pugnacious. Lobsters are often observed sparring with one another, with claws raised in front of them like two boxers in the ring. If one fighter gets the other in a claw-lock, the loser can "throw" (release) its claw and retreat. Being a cannibal, the winner will

The American lobster has two strong claws: a crusher claw and a ripper or pincher claw.

usually eat the claw its opponent just dropped. On the ocean bottom, lobsters may fight over shelters. In captivity, lobsters fight over which will become the boss of the tank. Losing lobsters will grovel or retreat from more dominant lobsters in the tank. Crowded into tight quarters, a lobster will attack and eat another lobster if given the chance, which is why lobsters are banded after being captured. Even when threatened by a much larger predator, such as a human or a cod, the lobster typically responds with an assertive snap of the claws and a powerful flick of its tail.

The lobster hides in a burrow by day and prowls the ocean floor under the cover of darkness. It only seeks the company of other lobsters when it wants to mate. Even though it prefers to live alone, it is also curious. When the lobster ventures out at night, it frequently snoops around the

Even this tiny New England lobster defends itself with spirit.

Sea urchins are among the many animals of the ocean floor that are eaten by lobsters.

burrows of neighboring lobsters. Once it makes sure that the resident isn't at home, it sneaks inside for a peek. If it likes what it sees, it may evict the former occupant when it returns the next morning. Sometimes a large lobster forces a smaller lobster out of its home apparently just for the sake of showing who's boss. The bullying lobster will back into the den, stay just a few minutes, and then exit and allow its original owner to return.

A lobster is voracious. It may attack and eat up to 100 different kinds of animals (and some plants). On the ocean floor, the lobster may cover a mile or more each night hunting for crabs, snails, mussels, starfish, and an occasional slow-moving flounder. It digs for clams, worms, and slender fish called sand lance.

The lobster does not really deserve its reputation as a scavenger. It prefers live prey to picking over the remains of someone else's meal. Some lobstermen claim that lobsters are attracted to old bait, the smellier the better, but there doesn't seem to be much truth to that. Fresh bait works at least as well and is much more pleasant to use!

These tiny lobsters, about a month or so old, have just changed from floating
plankton to bottom dwellers.

CHAPTER THREE
Lobster Lore

The lobster starts life as an egg no larger than the head of a pin. When it hatches about ten months later, it looks more like an insect than a lobster. (Lobstermen call lobsters "bugs.") Feathery hairs on its legs keep it suspended in the water for the first month or so after hatching. At this stage the tiny lobster floats near the surface of the sea as "plankton." It is unable to control or direct where it goes. Sometimes it bumps into something smaller that it can devour. If it encounters any sea

A lobster this size—approximately a year old—may survive if it stays in hiding for the next several years.

creatures bigger than itself, which is most of them, it will be eaten. Of 10,000 eggs that a young mother may carry, only ⅒ of one percent—maybe 10—will survive beyond their first four weeks of life. During that time, if it manages to escape being eaten, the baby lobster will molt, or shed its shell, three times before it begins to look like a miniature adult.

By then it is a "fourth-stage" lobster between fifteen days and a month old. It has lost the feathery appendages that kept it afloat, and its two front claws have grown heavy enough to drag it to the ocean bottom. It begins to seek out the darkness of the depths rather than the brightness of the surface waters. It may bob up and down in the water for a while, until, as a "fifth-stage" lobster the size of a penny, it takes to the bottom for good.

After it settles to the bottom, a small lobster still has many enemies.

All kinds of fishes, especially cod, as well as larger lobsters will attack it if it leaves its shelter. The tiny lobster spends the next few years, until it is almost four years old, hiding under seaweed and small rocks, catching food that drifts down to it. A small lobster rarely ventures out of hiding. If it does, it is attacked within minutes.

All the while the lobster continues to molt or shed its shell, up to twenty-five times in its first five years of life. Molting is hard work. First, the flesh inside the claws shrivels to about a quarter of its normal size. Then the old shell cracks along the joint that separates the carapace (the back shell) and the tail and along a line down the middle of its back. The lobster flexes its body several times to pull itself from the cracked shell.

Even though the claw muscles have shrunk, they sometimes get stuck in the narrow knuckle of the claw during molting. Then the lobster must

When a claw is lost, only a pink fleshy bud remains.

release the claw and abandon both the shell and flesh. It does this by forcefully squeezing a muscle that encircles the claw. This powerful muscle contraction releases the claw and seals the stump with hardly any loss of blood. The lost claw won't be replaced until the next molt; only a small pink fleshy bud marks the stump. (A lobster can release a claw at will, especially if it is threatened in a fight.)

Underneath the old shell is a wrinkled soft shell that will expand and harden into a new outer covering, complete with claws. While the new shell is still soft, the lobster absorbs seawater and gains about 15 percent in size and 40-50 percent in weight. A just-molted lobster feels like a rubber toy. If it is lifted from the support of the water, its heavy front claws may drop right off. It stays in hiding for a week or two until the new shell is fortified against predators. The lobster eats the old shell, which provides calcium to help harden the new one more quickly.

As lobsters reach legal size, males molt about once a year and females molt about every two years, usually in the summer. The shell remains thin for several weeks. The new shell is extra large, to accommodate the growing lobster for a year or more. Much of the weight of a "shedder," or newly molted lobster, is water, as disappointed diners who crack open one quickly learn. Yet many people prefer the sweet meat of a soft-shell lobster.

A lobster continues to grow throughout its life, although it molts less frequently as it grows older. The largest lobster ever caught was taken off Nova Scotia in 1977. It weighed 44 pounds, 6 ounces and was between three and four feet long. It may have been 100 years old. So many variables—water temperature, the amount of salt in the water, availability of shelter, depth of water—affect when a lobster will molt and grow that figuring out the age of any lobster is nothing more than an educated guess.

Like fish, frogs, and turtles, a lobster is a cold-blooded creature. Its

WORLD'S
RECORD
LOBSTER

One of the largest lobsters ever caught is displayed at the Museum of Science in Boston.

body takes on the temperature of its surroundings. The animal becomes more active when the temperature is warm; it slows down when the temperature drops. When the temperature of the seawater rises in summer, the lobster eats more, moves farther, and grows faster.

Lobsters migrate in response to changes in the water temperature. As a rule, a lobster moves nearer to shore in the warm weather (sometimes right up to the surf zone) and offshore to deeper water in the late fall and winter. Several lobstermen who fish the bays and nearshore waters of Maine claim their prey don't really move much at all seasonally. They say they just can't catch them in cold weather because the lobsters "numb up." The crustaceans show no interest in feeding and don't crawl into traps. They dig into the bottom, leaving only their eyes and antennae exposed, and stay in semihibernation until the coastal waters warm up in the spring to about 40°F. Offshore the water temperature doesn't decrease

A close-up of a lobster shows a face armored like a knight's helmet.

substantially, so the lobsters living in deeper water remain active throughout the winter.

Most lobsters don't move great distances during the course of their lives, probably no more than ten miles from where they settled down as baby lobsters. The few that do travel far tend to be large lobsters that live in deeper water. A few large lobsters, tagged for scientific study, traveled over 200 miles between where they were released and where they were recaptured.

A lobster paces the ocean bottom in a shadowy world where vision is not all that important. Each eye, set on a movable stalk, has up to 10,000 facets that operate like many tiny eyes. The lobster probably doesn't see images, but its eyes can detect motion in dim light. In bright light, a lobster is probably blind.

Instead, the lobster learns about its environment through touch, taste, and smell. In fact, you could say the lobster's whole body is a sense organ. The long pair of antennae and tiny hairs that cover the entire body, especially the walking legs, are sensitive to touch. Short bristles called "hedgehog hairs" line the insides of the pincers on the walking legs. These are akin to our taste buds, so a lobster can be said to taste with its feet. If it likes what it picks up, it passes the food along to its mouth where sensory bristles on its mouth parts also detect taste.

The shorter set of antennae—the antennules—perceive long-distance odors or chemical signals carried by the seawater. These "chemoreceptors" help a lobster find food, choose a mate, and decide whether to fight or flee. Delicate hairs on the antennules have more than 400 receptors, sensitive enough to distinguish between a horse mussel and a blue mussel, for instance. One researcher who has studied the senses of lobsters for over twenty years is Dr. Jelle Atema of the Boston University Marine Program at the Marine Biological Laboratory in Woods Hole, Massachu-

This magnified view of the antennules reveals the lobster's sensory hairs which can detect food, enemies, and potential mates.

setts. He is constantly amazed at how much information a lobster's chemical receptors can glean from the seawater. Says Dr. Atema, "They may enable the animals to detect the species, sex, and even the mood of another animal." If the antennules of a lobster are removed, it can find food only if it literally bumps into it.

A lobster is a messy eater. By the time it's done feeding there is usually a cloud of debris around it. After tearing apart its prey with its front claws, it uses its walking legs to move the pieces forward where its mouth parts hold the food and shred it. The food passes into a part of the stomach—the gastric mill—where three sets of grinding surfaces resembling human molars crush fish bones and shell fragments. You could say that a lobster chews with its stomach!

One place humans can easily study lobster anatomy is at the dinner table. The first thing to do when your cooked lobster arrives is turn it over to see if it is a male or female. The swimmerets, small feathery appendages on the tail, will provide the clue. The first pair of swimmerets closest to the body are hard and bony on a male, and soft and feathery, like the rest of the swimmerets, on a female.

The two large claws of the lobster (the parts most people eat first) are called *chelipeds*. Between the claws are the mouth parts, antennae, antennules, and rostrum or beak, all of which are inedible. After that, most people eat the tail which has small flippers or *telsons* at the base. The eight walking legs are also edible. Intrepid diners who explore further find small chunks of meat inside the carapace. They may also encounter gills, green "tomalley" (the digestive gland), and in a female, red "coral" or

The difference between a male and female lobster shows in the swimmerets, the feathery appendages on the underside of the tail. The first pair closest to the body are hard on a male (left photo), soft on a female (right photo).

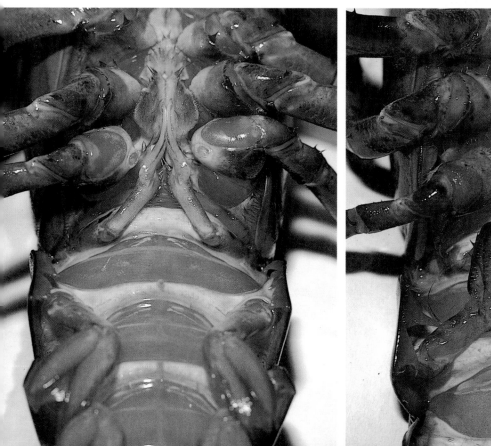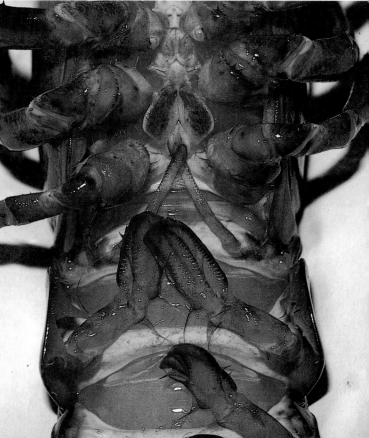

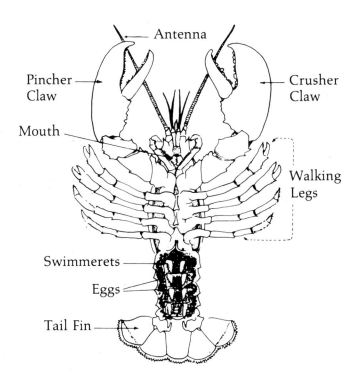

Lobster: Bottom view

"roe" (unfertilized eggs). Hard-core lobster lovers eat the latter two.

Although at the dinner table lobsters are red, the normal *living* lobster is greenish-black on top and orange below, with accents of blue on the joints of its claws. Its shell is composed of three pigments—red, blue, and yellow. When one or more of these pigments is missing at birth, a red, blue, albino (white), or calico (dark with yellow spots) color pattern results. Blue lobsters occur once in every 3-4 million lobsters. Red lobsters (live ones) occur once in every 10 million. Except for albinos, all the color variations of lobsters turn red when they are cooked.

A living lobster is greenish-black on top and orange below.

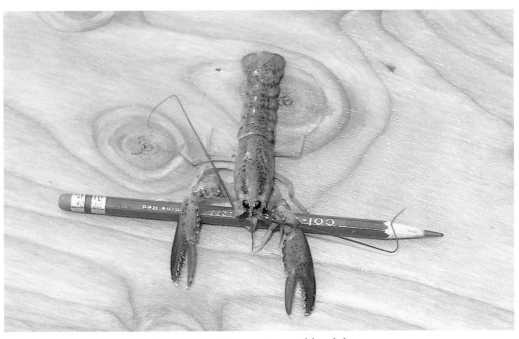

A rare genetic mutation: a blue lobster

A male lobster searches for a shelter in preparation for courtship and mating.

CHAPTER FOUR

Lobster Society

While a lobster may not be very sociable, lobster society—how they interact—is very complex. Most of what we know about lobster behavior has come from watching them in tanks in oceanographic laboratories. But researchers suspect that the behavior lobsters exhibit in captivity, like animals in the zoo, is not how they really behave on the ocean floor. To try to understand the true nature of these animals, some scientists have spent many hours underwater in shallow bays, watching lobsters and recording their actions play-by-play on plastic waterproof tablets or videotaping their interactions like an aquatic "Candid Camera."

DOMINANCE

Lobsters that live together soon establish a pecking order. They may fight once, sometimes with great ferocity, to determine who will become the boss. After that, whenever the two lobsters meet, the winner whips his antennae across the other lobster's claws. This action is a form of communication. The loser grovels in the sand until the dominant one passes by. The dominant lobster gets first choice of shelters, food, and mates. In captivity (and probably in nature as well), the female lobsters actually stagger their molts in order to wait their turn to mate with the dominant male.

COURTSHIP

Lobsters may be feisty, but they are tender lovers, claims Dr. Jelle Atema, who has studied lobster senses extensively. Because a female lobster mates only just after she sheds her corsetlike shell, it is a time when she is most vulnerable to attack from predators. In order to ensure a successful encounter between these potential cannibals, lobster society has evolved a complex courtship ritual. When she is ready to molt, the female lobster approaches a male's den (usually the largest male in the neighborhood). She wafts a "sex perfume" called a *pheromone* in his direction. He responds by fanning the water with his swimmerets, permeating his apartment with her scent. He emerges from his den with his claws raised. She responds with a brief boxing match or by turning away. Either attitude seems to work to convince the male of her amorous intentions. They enter the den together.

Some time after, from a few hours to several days later, the female raises her claws and places them on the head of the male, "knighting" him to let him know she is ready to molt and mate. At this point in the courtship, the male could mate with her or eat her, but he invariably does the noble thing. He gently turns her limp body over onto her back with

An average female lobster lays between 10,000 and 20,000 eggs at a time.

his walking legs and his mouth parts, being careful not to tear her soft flesh. They mate "with a poignant gentleness that is almost human," observes Dr. Atema. The male, which remains hard-shelled, inserts his first pair of swimmerets, which are rigid and grooved, and passes his sperm into a receptacle in the female's body. She stays in the safety of his den for about a week until her new shell hardens. By then the attraction has passed, and the couple part with hardly a backward glance.

The female stores the sperm for many months. When she is ready to lay her eggs, she turns onto her back and cups her tail. The eggs are fertilized as they are pushed from her ovaries. An average-size female will lay 10,000 to 20,000 eggs. A sticky substance cements them to her tail where she will protect them from predators for nine to eleven months until they hatch. When it's time for the eggs to hatch, the female lifts her tail into the current and sets them adrift in the sea. It may take up to two weeks for all of the eggs to be released. A lobster's pregnancy is long—from mating to hatching is perhaps twenty months—but after birth, the responsibilities of motherhood are over. The female is free to start scouting out her next romantic encounter, or simply to look for a good meal.

TRAP BEHAVIOR

Chances are she will find it in a lobster trap. One would expect a lobster, if it had ever been caught, to avoid lobster traps forevermore. But lobsters have been videotaped crawling into and out of lobster traps to feed on bait fish or stealing pieces of bait through the slats of the traps. Some lobsters picked up the cages and crawled underneath to reach the food. They even crawled into traps where there was no bait.

One study showed just how important lobster traps are as a food supply for lobsters. Forty-eight lobstermen voluntarily removed their traps for six weeks from a popular lobstering area along the Maine coast. Shortly after all the traps were removed from the fishing grounds, the lobsters left, too. Dr. Robert Steneck of the University of Maine concluded that baited lobster traps are an important source of food supply for lobsters and that at certain times of the year, lobsters feed more on handouts from lobstermen than on their natural prey.

A lobster boat loaded with gear heads out for a day at sea.

CHAPTER FIVE

The Society of the Lobsterman

The lobster trap is the direct connection between the lobsters' society and the society of lobstermen. A lobster trap is a wire or wooden affair with at least two compartments. The smell of bait lures the crustacean into the first chamber, the "kitchen," where the bait is hung from a bait bag which may consist of "cuttings" (heads and other unusable parts) of menhaden, herring, or redfish. Then the lobster may wander through another funnel into the "parlor" where it drops to the bottom of the trap and usually can't get out. Every trap must have an "escape vent," an opening near the bottom that resembles a mail slot. It allows lobsters that have not reached legal size to exit.

Most nearshore lobstermen set 300 to 800 traps for one or two nights, in depths of water ranging from five feet to 250 or 300 feet. An industrious lobsterman working with a sternman can bait and set about 300 traps in a day. If the weather is good, they can complete a circuit of all their traps every two or three days. One "string" of traps can hold as many as 40 traps on one line (15 to 20 traps per string is more common). The traps lie on the ocean floor about 60 feet apart. Lobster buoys are attached to either end of a string of traps to mark its location.

Most lobstermen start putting their traps in the water in late spring, and fish through the summer into late fall. When storms start to take their toll on the gear, most lobstermen haul out their traps for the winter and use the break to repair or replace traps and buoys or to fish for sea urchins, shrimp, or scallops.

Sometimes traps are separated from their buoys by storm waves or by boats cutting the lines that connect them. Then the traps are lost to the fisherman. Lobsters will continue to enter the pots and may become permanently trapped. To prevent lobsters from being imprisoned forever, an escape panel is built into each trap. A hinged door is fastened shut by a biodegradable ring. After six or seven months, the ring rusts and falls off, allowing an escape hatch to open. It is large enough so that even legal-size lobsters will be able to leave the "ghost trap."

Although the boundaries are invisible, every lobsterman has his own "territory" on the ocean floor. In most ports, lobstermen have an informal, often unspoken, agreement about where each member of the fishing community may lay his traps. In small, closely knit fishing villages, long-time residents claim and defend their fishing territories from lobstermen

A wooden lobster trap is hauled onto the railing of the boat.

from other harbors and from newcomers. Family connections are very important in deciding who will be allowed to lobster in an area. Youngsters who want to become lobstermen may start with a few traps or work as "sternmen," baiting traps and carting gear, for older fishermen. Eventually, after a suitable apprenticeship, they will be allowed to take over their own territories. Women often work on the boats as "sternmen" for their fathers or husbands. A few get to be captains of their own vessels. Many other women handle the business end of lobstering while their husbands fish. Lobstering "territories" not only ensure a continued livelihood for the members of a particular harbor, but they help to conserve the local lobster population from overfishing.

A young lobsterman learns the trade from his father.

A daughter helps tend traps with her father.

Stacking traps in preparation for Trap Day on Monhegan Island

In the isolated fishing community of Monhegan Island, ten miles off the coast of Maine, about 60 lobstermen have exclusive rights (by tradition, not law) to a two-mile radius of ocean around this rockbound island. The lobstering season on Monhegan runs from January 1 to June 25. The island is closed to lobstering (and open to tourism) the other six months of the year.

January 1 here is not the day after the celebration of the night before, but Trap Day, the launching of a new fishing year. At dawn, all the lobster boats leave the harbor together and continue to lobster throughout the worst weather and the highest lobster prices of the year. These lobstermen feel that their January-June fishing season protects the lobster population when it needs it most: in the summer when the animals are molting and mating.

Lobstermen's wives fill bait bags on Monhegan. At dawn on January 1 all the lobster boats leave the harbor together.

39

Other lobstering communities don't officially close their fishing season, but they all are conscientious about other conservation measures. All states now share the minimum legal size of 3¼ inches "carapace length"— measured between the eye socket and the beginning of the tail. A lobster caught at this size weighs about 1¼ pounds.

A lobster gauge lets the fisherman know if he can keep this lobster.

Smaller lobsters and any egg-bearing or "berried" females must be returned to the sea. A V-notched female with a slice cut from a tail flipper must also be released. Maine is the only state that imposes a maximum legal size (5 inches carapace length), so the "biggest breeders," which may produce 100,000 eggs rather than the average 10,000 eggs, can stay in the population.

A short lobster is returned unceremoniously, but unharmed, to the sea.

AQUACULTURE

Some of the money from the sale of lobster licenses in Maine goes to fund a "seed lobster program" to support research in aquaculture or "sea farming." Lobsters are not easy to raise in captivity, and as yet no one has made a profit from it. Lobsters are cannibalistic at all ages. As larvae, they are kept in large vats with whirlpool currents to keep the baby lobsters spinning beyond each other's grasp. When they settle to the bottom, they must be kept in individual pens and moved to ever-larger enclosures as they grow. Add in food costs (lobsters can be picky eaters in captivity), heating the water to make them grow faster, and treating disease, and it's easy to see why raising a lobster to adulthood is expensive.

When a Maine lobsterman finds a rare blue lobster in his trap, he is likely to bring it to Sam Chapman to use in breeding experiments.

Another approach to lobster aquaculture is to hatch the eggs and raise the lobsters only to their fourth or fifth stages when they start to settle to the bottom. Then the hatchery operators free the two-month-old lobsters into the ocean and hope that they survive long enough to join the lobster fishery as market-size catch. But how do we know if it works? That is a question that aquaculturist Sam Chapman at the University of Maine's Darling Research Center has been trying to answer by raising blue lobsters, the offspring of a blue mother and a blue father. He raises the baby blues to their fourth stage and releases them at two sites along the Maine coast. If even only 3 percent of these blue lobsters show up in lobster traps near the release sites in five to seven years, his efforts to add laboratory-raised lobsters to Nature's supply will have paid off. Perhaps someday we will see blue lobsters sold in the supermarket next to the dark ones. Before that day, one more bit of research is required. Because blue lobsters are so rare, no one has yet tried cooking and eating one to see if it tastes as good as a normal one!

A chef at Jimmy's Harborside Restaurant in Boston drops a live lobster into the steaming pot.

CHAPTER SIX

Eating Lobsters: A Lobster's Fate

Lobster is one of the few restaurant items in which you are encouraged to choose your own individual victim. (There are some restaurants in the Midwest where you can pick out your own steak, but it's not like seeing the whole cow.) This places a heavy responsibility (and guilt) on the diner. Should you have a soft-shell or a hard-shell lobster? Should you choose a male or a female? Should you buy a "chicken" (1 pound), a "deuce" (2 pounds), or a "jumbo" (2½ to 4 pounds)?

Bright red lobsters are ready to serve.

According to David Dow, Director of the Lobster Institute in Orono, Maine, and a lobsterman himself, "Most people in the industry prefer the new shell—the 'shedders.' Their meat is sweet, and the shells are easy to break apart." Dow also claims that large lobsters taste as good as small ones "until you get to 5 to 7 pounds. Then the meat gets kind of stringy." As for sex, advocates of tail meat recommend getting a female, because her tail is broader than a male's of equal size, since she needs the space to carry her eggs.

Because lobster meat can spoil quickly, it's generally necessary to cook a lobster while it's still alive. How to do that in the most humane manner has been a concern of guilt-ridden chefs for generations. In order to put the matter to rest scientifically, one researcher ordered his graduate students to boil lobsters after having subjected them to various techniques designed to relax the lobsters. The students determined which method killed kindest by counting the number of tail flicks heard in the kettle before each lobster succumbed to the boiling water. They tried hypnotizing the lobsters (rubbing their backs until they stood on their heads), soaking them in fresh water, heating the water slowly from room temperature to boiling, and other accepted strategies. They found that putting them in the refrigerator before cooking to numb them up (like in winter) resulted in the lowest number of tail twitches. So, according to modern science, a few minutes in the freezer means less agony in the kettle.

Communities like Monhegan Island depend on a stable supply of lobsters to continue their way of life.

CHAPTER SEVEN

The Future of the Lobster and the Lobsterman

Lobstering has been an industry only since about 1800. Before that, in colonial times, lobsters were considered "poverty food" or used for fertilizer. Large lobsters could be harvested from the rocky shore at low tide. They were served to children, to prisoners, and to indentured servants, who had exchanged their passage to America for seven years of service to their sponsors. Finally, some of the indentured servants rebelled. They had it put into their contracts that they would not be forced to eat lobster more than three times a week.

Cape Codders in Massachusetts were the first to start a commercial fishery for lobsters around 1810. As landlubbers in New York and Boston began to develop a taste for the crustaceans, lobster harvesting began to expand northward to meet the demand. By 1840, Maine had developed a lobster fishery, and Canada followed by 1870. By the 1880s, overfishing was becoming such a problem that laws regulating lobstering were passed.

Today's lobstermen are landing more pounds of lobsters than their fathers did a generation ago. In fact, in the past few years, New England lobstermen have had their highest annual landings ever: 35-45 million pounds valued at $100 million. Yet the number of lobstermen catching those lobsters has more than doubled, which means that each lobsterman gets fewer lobsters than a generation ago.

The lobsters that were caught a generation ago were much bigger. Over the years, the size of the average lobster has dropped dramatically from several pounds to barely 1 to 1½ pounds. Most lobsters are taken as soon as they reach legal size (they may have been caught in traps many times before then but were released). Even though the minimum legal size of lobsters was recently increased from 3³⁄₁₆ inches to 3¼ inches, most lobsters are removed from the sea before they have had a chance to reproduce even once. Along the Maine coast, only 5 to 6 percent of lobsters are sexually mature, or old enough to mate, when they reach the legal size of 3¼ inches. (In warmer waters more mature at a smaller size.)

Is the lobster population in danger because more lobsters are being caught now than ever before? Or do the large lobster catches of recent years indicate that there are more lobsters in the sea than ever before? No one seems to know the answer.

Why are lobstermen doing so well? There are several theories, all guaranteed to generate controversy wherever there are two or more lobstermen:

A just-caught lobster on the deck of a Maine lobster boat. How many more are left in the sea?

Global warming. The water temperature along the Maine coast has increased significantly over the past few years. Are lobsters being attracted closer to shore by the warmer temperatures?

Fewer predators. Cod, the lobster's main enemy under the sea, is much less abundant than it used to be because of overfishing by ground fishermen, those who drag nets across the ocean floor for bottom-dwelling fish, such as cod, haddock, and flounder.

Better detection. Modern electronics that can virtually "see" underwater are standard on most lobster boats. It can identify bottom type, topography, and depth, making the lobster's haunts easier to locate.

More fishermen. When there are more lobstermen, it stands to reason there will be higher catches, although each fisherman gets a smaller slice of the pie.

Will our grandchildren be able to have lobster on their dinner tables in the twenty-first century? Probably. The answer lies in continued research, conservation, and cooperation among lobstermen, scientists, and those who regulate the industry. We still have much more to learn about these "bugs" of the sea that taste so good.

Bibliography

ADULT TITLES

Acheson, James. *Lobster Gangs of Maine.* University Press of New England, Hanover, NH, 1988.

Ballenger, Bruce. *The Lobster Almanac.* The Globe Pequot Press, Chester, CT, 1988.

Brown, Allen D. *The Great Lobster Chase: The Real Story of Maine Lobsters and the Men Who Catch Them.* International Marine Publishing Co., Camden, ME, 1985.

Dueland, Joy. *The Book of the Lobster.* New Hampshire Publishing Co., Somersworth, NH, 1973.

Merriam, Kendall. *The Illustrated Dictionary of Lobstering.* The Cumberland Press, Freeport, ME, 1978.

Taylor, Herb. *The Lobster: Its Life Cycle.* Pisces Books, New York, 1984.

White, Susan, ed. *A Lobster in Every Pot: More Than Just A Cookbook.* Yankee Books, Camden, ME, 1990.

BOOKS FOR YOUNG READERS

Bailey, Jill. *Discovering Crabs and Lobsters.* Franklin Watts, New York, 1987.

Bayer, Robert and Juanita Bayer. *Lobsters Inside-Out.* Acadia Press, Bar Harbor, ME, 1989.

Harriman, Edward. *Leroy the Lobster and Crabby Crab.* Down East Books, Camden, ME, 1967.

Headstrom, Richard. *All About Lobsters, Crabs, Shrimps, and Their Relatives.* Dover Publications, New York, 1985.

Ipcar, Dahlov. *The Lobsterman.* Down East Books, Camden, ME, 1977.

McMillan, Bruce. *Finest Kind O' Day: Lobstering in Maine.* Lippincott, New York, 1977.

Index